T0208705

Crap Rolls Downhill, Plus Twenty-Four Other
Rules That Will Help Make You…

The Street-Smart Manager

Michael A. Fishman

iUniverse, Inc.
New York   Bloomington

Crap Rolls Downhill, Plus Twenty-Four Other
Rules That Will Help Make You...
The Street-Smart Manager

iUniverse books may be ordered through booksellers or by contacting:

iUniverse
1663 Liberty Drive
Bloomington, IN 47403
www.iuniverse.com
1-800-Authors (1-800-288-4677)

*Because of the dynamic nature of the Internet, any Web addresses or links contained in this book
may have changed since publication and may no longer be valid. The views expressed in this work
are solely those of the author and do not necessarily reflect the views of the publisher, and the
publisher hereby disclaims any responsibility for them.*

ISBN: 978-1-4401-7159-8 (pbk)
ISBN: 978-1-4401-7161-1 (ebook)

Printed in the United States of America

iUniverse rev. date: 10/8/09

So you wanted to be the manager? Then you no doubt learned that time is one of our most precious commodities. It is something we cannot afford to waste. If you think you know everything about managing, then don't take the time to read this book. If you think you can still become a better manager, then this book is for you. At the conclusion of my first official speaking seminar, one participant handed me a short note that said, "When a man with experience meets a man with money, the man with the experience walks away with the money; and the man with the money walks away with the experience." I think that says it all.

ACKNOWLEDGMENTS

I believe we must always learn from others, and it is sometimes easy to forget those who helped you along the way.

The short list of individuals below includes my role models for various traits important in my own growth as a person and as a manager.

- Harold Fishman. As a retail businessman, he taught me about honesty. Harold also taught me the lessons about the customer always being right and how important it is to do the right thing. In a small family-owned business, there is no substitute for a good reputation.
- Kermit Miller. The fact that his brother was Arthur Miller and his ex-sister-in-law was Marilyn Monroe had nothing to do with my respect for Kermit (although it did make knowing him even more interesting). He was the first manager who recognized my potential and encouraged me to be all that I hoped to be. He was my role model for integrity and class.
- Rick Jarit. Rick is my mentor and friend and was the epitome of a manager who had presence. He knew how to create relationships with his customers. He was a guy you wanted watching your back in your foxhole. Rick made me realize how

it important it is to compliment people when they do a good job.

- Alan Braunstein. Alan was the first person who gave me authority to make decisions where I did not have to worry about being second-guessed. He was a great example of the value of promotions and of embracing creativity. He showed me that first class was the best class.

- Jeffrey Lubinsky. Jeffrey was the best teacher of knowing how to run a big business. He knows how to survive in corporate America. He understands the value in making tough decisions while being fair to those important to the overall success of the mission. "It is what it is" states the corporate philosophy.

- Cyril Greenstein. The one thing I learned from Cy was not to be afraid of being theatrical. Put on a great show. His sales meetings got your attention and sent the right message to motivate the troops.

- Pat Shaw. Pat was a manager who stressed the virtues of strategic planning. He showed me how to prepare and be ready for anything that could arise. I observed and learned how to look at the whole picture and how thorough you had to be to get it right.

- Mike Satriano. Mike showed me the importance of product knowledge and how to be a professional salesperson. This professionalism taught me another level of salesmanship, which helped me become a better manager.

- Sonna Calandrino. Sonna was the key person to make me aware of a woman's view in business. She validated my creative talent and helped teach me the world of marketing. Sonna made me realize that the people who believe in what they are doing and who take a chance are the only individuals with any chance at winning.

- Bobby Bornstein. Bobby was the perfect example of a nice guy who knew how to win. I will always remember his great attitude and friendship. Billy Joel was right, "Only the good die young."

- David Engel. I will just keep this as simple as I can and simply state, "That's what friends are for." You will learn more from people's actions than you will from their words.
- Sam Allman. Sam and members of the Mohawk University training programs made me realize again the importance of education. He reminded me that we all benefit from learning and, more importantly, that we need to share this knowledge with others. He inspired me to write this book.
- I would like to acknowledge everybody that was there for me when I needed them.

INTRODUCTION

In 1981, my dreams and aspirations of becoming a sales manager came true. I was thirty-eight years old and the first person ever promoted to the position of sales manager from within my company. That was quite an accomplishment considering that the thirty-seven-year-old company was a dominant floor covering distributor in the New York metropolitan area. There were seventeen other salesmen in the company, and I was among the youngest members of this group. Besides my relative youth, I was definitely considered a lot less seasoned. I had exactly five years of experience as a salesman in my Brooklyn territory. Yet I had achieved some unbelievable sales results and was, indeed, the shining star of the sales staff.

Two of the three existing managers campaigned hard with the owners to convince them that my time had come. The third, the vice president of sales, sarcastically referred to me as "Golden Boy." I still remember being called into the owners' office, and both owners, a father and his son, congratulated me warmly as the new manager for the Hard Surface Flooring Division. I received my nonnegotiable salary deal, with expenses, which was not much more than my sales income. But I was still floating. As far as I was concerned, they could have cut my salary if my business cards came out looking pretty.

I remember only one thing that the owners said to me during that meeting. "We are paying you to make decisions. Don't be afraid of making them." With those words of enlightenment, I left the office with the best advice I had ever received.

The next day, I decorated my office with all my plaques and awards. I went through all the files and set up all my systems. I watered my new "congratulations" plant, and I sat behind my desk and said, "Okay, big shot, now what are you supposed to do?"

I didn't have a clue. It seems to me that the number-one method of training new managers is osmosis—the gradual, often unconscious, absorption of knowledge or ideas through continual exposure rather than deliberate learning.

How organized are you at training your new management? This book's purpose is to give you the guidelines on how to be a manager. To be a good manager, you have to think like a manager. You wouldn't go to law school merely to study and learn lots of laws and legal decisions of many overturned and outdated cases. The ultimate goal would be to teach you how to think and perform like a lawyer. My ultimate goal is to get you to think and perform like a manager. The simple rules and anecdotes in this book will help you begin to think like a manager. They reflect my experiences over the past twenty-five years. You and your current managers and mentors can use your own experiences that you feel are relevant to the topics. Many times, there are no right or wrong answers to these issues, and this is what decision-making is all about—making a decision even when there are no clear-cut answers. Somewhere along the line you will have to make a decision to have a plan to train your managers.

This book deals with how you can make the right decision. The best decision I ever made was to become a sales manager. My second-best decision was writing down everything I ever learned about decision making and what went into that philosophy. I may be unable to help you acquire these rules by just reading this simple book, but I do have the lofty goal of making you aware that these rules exist. So many salespeople aspire to management as their dream career. Once you are in the position, be sure it is a dream for you and not a nightmare for others. Remember that experience is learning from all your bad decisions. (Anyone who knows me will acknowledge that I have a lot of experience.)

At this point, I should mention that I never considered myself a natural-born salesperson. I started my professional career as a teacher in the Bedford-Stuyvesant section of Brooklyn in the New York City public school system. I taught for eight years in an elementary school that was rated one of the ten worst schools in the city. To attract teachers to work in this school, the district gave you job deferment status with the draft board. This was a great incentive for a professional student like me with almost eight years of college deferments. While I have some book smarts, it was my strong street-smarts that helped me survive and succeed in this very difficult environment. I carried this asset with me when I decided to become a commissioned salesman.

But I needed to find ways to express myself in a more competitive environment with larger monetary rewards. It was an extremely difficult decision, and there was a lot of family opposition. But I had to do what I thought was the right thing for me. I had some sales experience working in my family's retail store within the flooring industry. I thought I could do well because I felt that the real stuff in business happens on the street. It was my element.

Once I was promoted to manager, I learned a lot of hard life lessons. I believe these lessons, my rules of management, will not only help you make decisions with more confidence as a manager but also will lend some strong guidance for your new professional life. I am putting down one key rule for each year of my management career. It will take you about one hour to gain about fifty thousand hours of my practical knowledge and hard-earned street lessons. Most of us start out street-stupid; and from those experiences, we eventually get our street-smarts. From where I come from, it's an offer you can't refuse.

I have written this training manual in the same style I write my memos and letters, short and sweet and without fanfare. This way, you'll be able to glean from the lessons easily. The successful manager must be an excellent communicator and presenter. You will continually be judged on your presentation skills. The rest of this page is blank for a reason.

Contents

Rule #1: Crap Rolls Downhill.

On the list of seven words that you can't use on the radio or on television—unimaginable as it seems to me—"shit" is still one of them. Many comedians have used this prohibition in some really good material. We are, however, allowed to say crap because John Crapper is credited with popularizing the flushable toilet. For anyone who works for someone else, especially in a mid or large sized corporation, I would encourage you to use the word crap over shit; it means the same thing and is less offensive.

You all know very well that crap happens every day. There is no way around the bull crap. You have to be aware of the chain of command. For example, let's say that something is not going well for your region compared to the rest of the country. Let's say it is the sale of a new product. The corporate bigwigs point this out to the regional vice presidents. The regional vice presidents vehemently point this out to the general sales managers. The general sales managers very vehemently point this out to the district sales managers. The district sales managers most vehemently point this out to the territory managers … and ad infinitum down the chain of command. Once you understand this idea, you will know what is on the corporate radar and make the right decision to keep passing this crap down the line until it reaches the lowest level. The responsibility for the mechanics of a particular job keeps getting shoveled further and further down the chain of command.

This makes it easy for a manager to say, "I don't have crappy products; I just have crappy salespeople."

As a manager, be prepared for the pressure of getting the job done. The manager not only has to pass along the corporate message but also has to give direction to staff on completing the task. When it is your turn to apply the pressure, that is when your job begins. You have to have the ability to get your message out and figure out the ways to get the job done. You have to roll up your sleeves, grab a shovel, and get dirty. The further down the line you are, the dirtier you will get. If you don't understand this kind of crap, you will be shit out of luck. There's no better way to say it.

Rule #2: Ask for HELP.

I have come up with an easy formula to remember when you make decisions. Just ask yourself for HELP to become a CEO.

H—Be Honest.
E—Be Empathetic.
L—Be Logical.
P—Be Practical.

By getting this HELP, you will become consistent, effective, and organized. You will have the ingredients to become a CEO. It's really basic if you are aware of the challenge to excel. Be consistent in all your decision-making steps, and you will usually do well. At least you will know how you arrived at your decisions and can adjust when the formula needs alteration. Sometimes, you might have to adjust one of these principles, especially when the practical rule becomes the dominant factor in your decision-making equation. Sometimes, you just have to do something that gets you the business or desired results you are striving for. The only principle that you should never bend is honesty. When dealing with people, it is hard to say you are *pretty* or *fairly* honest. What does that mean? What about tactical exaggeration?

We all tend to exaggerate, but we have to realize the boundaries of when that exaggeration becomes nothing more than out-and-out fabrication. Fabrication is a fancy, sugarcoated way of *telling lies*.

Never put yourself in a position where you get caught in a lie. If you try to be 100 percent honest, then you will pass the test. For example, I had a manager whom I noticed was constantly caught in lies or misinformation. (Misinformation is another form of fabrication.) I came to realize that, whenever he would begin an explanation with the words "To be perfectly honest" or "The truth of the matter is," what he was saying was probably a cover-up for one or more lies. As street-smart as I thought I was, it only took me about five years to figure this rule out. If you are dishonest, this rule won't HELP you in the end.

Rule #3: "If it is to be, it is up to me."

This statement has served as the backbone of my philosophy in life. These ten two-letter words say it all. I remember where and when I first heard them as if it were yesterday. It was 1977 at my first Manufacturers' Convention in Washington, DC. I had been a distributor salesman for less than one year. I was bemoaning my fate and bad timing for my hire for the Brooklyn New York territory. If I had only been hired a few months sooner, I could have had the rich suburbs of Nassau County, Long Island. I was hoping that the person who got that lush job would fail so that I could get his job.

But when the motivational speaker spoke those ten little words at the conference, my life changed. It was then that I realized the only way I was going to change anything was to make the best of what I had. No longer was the sky going to open up and shower me with riches and rewards. The only person who was going to get me to the top was "me." I set my goals as high as I could dream, and I got there. And I got there with such speed and achievement that I became a manager exactly five years from my date of hire. After a couple of years as manager, I had to change one word of that maxim: "If it is to be, it is up to *us*."

What an important lesson that one-word change can make. When you become a manager, the first thing that you have to realize is that, no matter how good a salesperson you might have been or how successful you think you were, you are now going to be dependent on the people you manage. Henry Ford said it best. He called it the three p's—people, product, and prices. Just remember that people come first. You will not be a good manager—let alone a great one—if you do not have the right people. Hiring, training, and retaining the right people are your foremost jobs; recognizing when to let someone go is your second job. Awareness of the importance of this undertaking is critical to success. Experience by trial and error usually is the best teacher of these lessons. It is always a work in progress. Be sure you wear your hard hat.

Rule #4: Learn How to Delegate Authority.

To grow in any business you must learn to delegate authority. If you cannot do that, you will be mired in a sea of minutiae. Again, it all comes down to having the right people. Somewhere in your mind-set, you have to get past the idea that you are the only person who can do the job right. I have observed many overworked and befuddled people who cannot trust anyone else to do the job. They may be successful people, but they are not maximizing their opportunities. Being a manager is like network marketing. Put the network in place and manage it. Give those who work for you the opportunity to gain your trust. Give them meaningful responsibility, and let them share the load. If you try to do everything yourself, you are not a manager.

While I attended college, I worked during my summer vacations as a counselor at an overnight camp. The last week of the season was devoted to splitting the camp into two equal teams to play against each other in all forms of competition from sports to spelling bees. We called it "Color War," and it was as intense a rivalry as anyone could imagine. During my second year at the camp, I was selected to be a "general," a leader of one of the two teams. My team ultimately lost the war, and we were heartbroken. After the final event, the camp director took me aside and told me that I was the most talented counselor he had ever come across in all his years of camping. He said that, when he drew up the staffing for both teams, he tried his best to stack the deck against mine to make the sides more even. He then delivered an unbelievable message to a twenty-year-old kid. He said that the only reason we lost was because I tried do everything myself.

Evidently, I didn't have the confidence to trust others to do the tasks as well as I could. It was a lesson that has stayed with me forever. In the next three years, I never lost a color war again. I also learned what it took to be an effective manager. Once you can trust others to do what you ask, you have a team. A team is much more powerful than an individual. The sooner you give up the idea that you are the only person capable of doing something, the stronger the collective effort becomes. Empowering and trusting people are essential when you delegate authority. Giving people their rewards and recognition on a regular basis are key ingredients to your success. Never underestimate the power of an "attaboy" or an "attagirl."

Rule #5: There Is Nothing More Than 100 Percent.

When people tell me they give 110 percent to something, I am unimpressed. We all have heard people say, "One thing you know about me is that I give 110 percent!" If someone can give 110 percent, why can't they give 120 percent? Or 130 percent?

Keep it simple. Use a scale of one to one hundred, with one hundred as the highest score. If you give it everything you have, you are giving 100 percent. I have always considered myself the kind of person who gave the things I cared about, like my job, 100 percent. Like most of you, I am driven to be the best.

The biggest thing that keeps changing in the world is that we keep raising the bar for success. We keep redefining what it takes to reach 100 percent. In this new corporate technological revolution, we all work as hard and as long as we can. This is no great secret. Whatever you thought was 100 percent is still 100 percent. One hundred percent is what you perceive as giving everything you have. It just seems as though this "everything" is getting to be more and you have to figure out how to manage it.

But there are still only twenty-four hours in each day. How much more can you actually do? At what point can't you do anymore? At what point do you want to stop doing more? When you have done all you can, you've done enough. Dedicated, proud workers who want to be the best at what they do and who become top performers will consistently give all they can to their jobs. These top performers determine for themselves the limits to that dedication. Working as smart as they can is better than working as long as they can. Figuring out how to take some breaks is not a sin. Don't feel guilty when you goof off a little. Without that downtime, you can't operate at 100 percent.

Rule # 6: Being Nice Isn't Bad.

Leo Durocher, a colorful baseball manager in the 1940s and 1950s, coined the phrase "Nice guys finish last." It is amazing to me how many people quote and believe in that statement. I am offended by people who believe in that credo. There is nothing wrong with being "nice." I believe many of the "good guys" are the biggest winners.

I worked for a small but very financially successful flooring distributor. It was a father-and-son team. The son was as "nice" a person as you could ever meet, and the eighty-year-old father was a modern-day Simon Legree. Whenever you asked the son how business was, he jokingly said, "It starts out slow in the morning and then tapers off in the afternoon." The father's standard line was, "Business is fine. That Mike Fishman has made me a millionaire. Unfortunately, before he teamed up with my son, I was a multimillionaire."

But trust me—the son was the real winner. There is nothing wrong with having empathy and concern for the people you work with. Being a good person will get you a lot further in the long run. If you have all the tools to be a great manager and you manage with empathy, you will achieve success with the respect and loyalty of your staff. Being a "nice" person doesn't mean that you can't or don't make tough decisions. It doesn't mean you aren't ultra-competitive and willing to do whatever it takes to win—other than cheating. If you have to cheat or play dirty to win, then you are a loser.

As a manager, one of my goals is to have those around me work under the best possible conditions. They will perform much better in a positive, sincere, caring environment. It is good to have the respect of those who work for and with you. It is even better to be liked and respected.

Don't abuse the word "boss." I actually don't respond well when someone refers to me as his or her boss. At times, I have had a combined staff of more than one hundred managers and salespeople working with me. As the general sales manager of that group, I prefer to think of myself as their leader. They all have the ability to be heard and to contribute to the decision-making process. I don't want to be their boss. I want to be the manager and the leader. I want to be the one who measures their results and helps everyone achieve our mutual goals. Like Ensign Pulver in *Mister Roberts,* just remember that, as a manager, you are "in charge of laundry and morale."

Rule #7: Obey All Rules.

I probably could have made this rule number one, but it really doesn't matter. All of these rules can be rule number one. About forty years ago on *The Andy Griffith Show*, there was an episode in which Deputy Barney Fife was put in charge of watching the local jail and its one prisoner, the town drunk. In his toughest pose, the inept Fife explained to the man, "We only have one rule here in this here Mayberry Jail, and that is to obey all rules." It sounds easy to remember, and I still do remember it.

The same thing is true in large or small businesses. Contrary to the popular notion that "rules are meant to be broken," you are now one of the guardians of those rules as a manager. Records are made to be broken. Rules are made to be followed. There is a fine line between knowing how to perform within the system by getting around the red tape and breaking the rules. Whenever you process information to make a decision, be sure you stay within the guidelines of what you know is right. If you cannot make a decision that you can share openly with your supervisors, then you are probably making the wrong decision. Rules can be changed or altered. Good managers know how to change rules and the system itself. Be watchful of those who think they can break rules with impunity. Learn how to work within the rules, and you will be golden.

Rule #8: If You Want to Have a Good Memory, Write It Down.

We are all wrapped up in so much day-to-day interaction that it is easy to have selective memory. When I was younger, we had a standing line about certain people: "He has a good memory, but it's short."

Documenting important business decisions and transactions in writing is pragmatic in order to avoid controversy. I had a manager who had a tendency to get into trouble. Whenever I confronted him about the difference between what he said and what the customer claimed he said, his response was, "But I wrote it down in my notebook." (I had no idea if he actually wrote it down at the time of the event, after the event, or not at all. Most of the time, I was talking to him on the telephone while he could have been reading a magazine.) The reality was that, even if what he said was true, he was the only one with a record of that conversation. If it is important information, then it must be distributed to the other people involved. After several confrontations involving that manager over what was said, I instructed him to put everything in writing and copy everyone involved.

We all can have selective memories. People often only hear what they want to hear. Maybe we do it on purpose, or maybe it is just part of human nature. A famous philosopher once said that the secret to happiness is good health and a short memory. This may not hold so true in today's high-tech society. One of the new catchphrases used daily in my organization is *crystal clear*, meaning emphatically, leaving no doubt about what you are saying.

Be certain people acknowledge all the facts as presented. They don't have to agree with your opinions, but there must be full understanding of the issue or the task. Am I being crystal clear? If not, I will say it again. If you want to have a good memory, write it down.

Do you think you can remember that?

Rule #9: Always Be Punctual.

Nothing can be more frustrating than waiting for someone who is late. In many ways, it is a sign of rudeness—as if your time isn't as valuable as mine. The very act of deciding what time to set your alarm clock or when to leave for an appointment is as important as any other. It takes careful planning and calculation.

Several years ago, I was listening to a radio talk show, and the topic of stress came up. According to a study in England, the number one cause of stress was getting to work on time. Picture the average clock-puncher's high stress level doing everything as frantically or as organized as possible to get there before work begins. That stress intensifies when complications, like a traffic jam or missed connection, come into play. What about when you go downstairs to your car; and just as you're about to leave, you realize you forgot something (like your car keys or cell phone)? Or you get a last-minute phone call? Those small or large time eaters are serious stress enhancers.

According to British survey, if you allowed fifteen more minutes of extra time just to get to work, you would live two to three years longer. In other words, if your goal is to catch the 7:37 morning train for the city, do not try to get to the station at 7:36 AM. When you are punctual, people can depend on you. Don't be lumped into that group of "Oh, he's always late." That is a poor group to be in, and I won't accept that as someone's practice. I make it my business to try to leave lots of extra time to account for SNAFUs (situation normal all fouled up) and complications. It is comforting and takes that stress of being on time out of the equation.

If someone works for me, he or she will learn to arrive early. My time is too valuable to be spent waiting in a parking lot for someone to show up. By the way do you know the number two cause of the most stress in an average person's life? Some of my managers might say, "Not being late for Fishman's meetings." The actual answer from the survey was, going on vacation. Just picture the old O. J. running through the airport to catch a plane. It *Hertz* a little to use him as an example but he is still the perfect visualization of someone running through an airport. By the way, if you plan to take your laptop, BlackBerry, cell phone, and other business-related techno-toys, you have already sullied the word "vacation." Just make up your mind that when you return from vacation you will be coming home on what I have termed as E-Day. A day of looking at hundreds of e-mails that managed to survive your lack of attention even while you were away. Taking a real vacation, without all your business toys, is nonnegotiable. This is a law, not a rule.

Rule #10: Learn from Others.

When I interview people, I examine their work history with a very keen eye. Some may look at people with a long resume of jobs and changes and see only negatives. Often, we say these people have some baggage. I see it in a much different light from that obvious deduction. Very often, this baggage can turn out to be designer luggage. When someone has had a successful career with several different companies, this can be a good thing. In many ways, the experience this person has gained working in different organizations can prove invaluable. On the other hand, the person who has the stability of working for one company for twenty-five years typically only knows that company's way of doing business.

I have worked in several organizations of various sizes and stature. I have worked for and with many owners, salespeople, and managers. I can proudly say that I have taken a great deal of knowledge and character traits from many of those colleagues. There are so many practical lessons you can learn from different people with a range of backgrounds. As a manager and a person, you will come to decide which character strengths to incorporate into your own style and which traits are weaknesses, which you will try to avoid. Study the people you currently work with. Think about all the people you've met, and try to identify the people you would like to use as role models. Maybe there was only one thing about them that stands out. What was it they did that you can take away from that experience and put on paper? Identifying the positive and negative influences in your life helps you see where you are and how you got there. In many ways, you will become a character witness. I acknowledge individuals who helped me at the beginning of the book.

Rule #11: Understand the Rule of Thumb.

You might, as I do, hear people often say, "as a rule of thumb, this is how I do" some task. What exactly is that person saying, and how does that apply to decision making?

A rule of thumb is a vague guide to what you normally would do given a similar set of circumstances. The saying comes from Old English law where it was written "that a husband could beat his wife with a stick no wider than his thumb." As a manager, there are many times that you will find yourself using that saying. (You probably would also like to flog some of your staff from time to time if it were legal.)

In your own situation and circumstances, you will create your own catalogue of rules and their applications. Your subordinates will expect the rules to be logical and consistent but not written in stone. They will become something your employees can rely on. The good part about rules of thumb is that the rules are simply a guide and are more flexible than written rules. As a rule of thumb, for example, whenever there is an opportunity to promote someone from within the company, I want to do it. It is a good reward for the employee's loyalty and past performance. It is a great tool for nurturing morale for the individual and for the organization. People who want to be promoted find ways of letting you know and do their own form of campaigning. People who are more talented than others seem to rise above the crowd without advertisement. Given a close decision between a current employee and a candidate from the outside, I go with my present employee. However, if that outsider is clearly the stronger candidate, I alter my decision in favor of the external candidate who brings the most to the table. That is my rule of thumb.

A rule of thumb is a guideline, not a written rule. I can make a logical decision to go in another direction from that guideline. People in my company know that I am consistent in my thinking. They have come to understand how I operate. They may not be able to put into words everything that happens, but they understand it when it occurs. As a rule of thumb, I generally don't change my rules of thumb. As a rule of thumb, I generally don't verbalize the words "rule of thumb" since I don't like the connection of hitting one's wife with a stick.

RULE #12: KNOW THE DIFFERENCE BETWEEN FACT AND OPINION.

One serious problem people encounter is separating fact from fiction or fact from opinion. I write this down without a safety net or reference guide because these are the facts the way I know them. This is just my street talk. Fiction is something that somebody creates or makes up and therefore is not true. I have to be sure to eliminate all fiction from my decision-making process in order to make solid, tenable decisions because fiction cannot be verified as truth—it's largely or entirely made up.

A good decision is not necessarily the right decision. It is, however, the best decision you can make based on the facts you know. People make most decisions based on opinions as well as facts. When you make a decision, gather your facts and make the best decision you can. You are offering your opinion based on the facts. But be sure not to make decisions without evidence or verification (i.e., fiction). A fact is something that cannot be argued. Once we have agreed on the terminology, facts by themselves are irrefutable. It is a fact that George Herman "Babe" Ruth hit 60 home runs for the New York Yankees in 1927. It is a documented irrefutable fact. George Herman "Babe" Ruth was the greatest baseball player of all time. That is an opinion. You can give all the statistics you want to back up that opinion, but it will always be an opinion. Remember that a statistic is a numerical fact.

People take these statistics and spin them any way they want to arrive at their own conclusions. At the time of this writing Wayne Gretzky has the highest point total in National Hockey League history. That is a fact. Wayne Gretzky is the greatest hockey player of all time. That is an opinion. Tiger Woods is the greatest golfer on the world tour for 2007 and 2008. Is that a fact or opinion? When you are making a decision, gather your facts and make the best decision you can. You are offering your opinion based on the facts. If all you had were easy decisions, it would be hard to call them decisions. That's my opinion of that. When a doctor makes a diagnosis, in reality he is offering an opinion. He is using his medical skills and experience to arrive at a logical conclusion. Would you want the first-year practitioner or the Harvard-trained old-timer? That is why many people seek second opinions. It is easy to diagnose a broken wrist if you look at an X-ray and it shows the bone is broken. Doctors may differ as to the best procedure for mending it, but they would agree on the fact that it is broken. A hundred doctors could examine the wrist without an X-ray and say it is not broken. They all would be wrong if one doctor showed them the X-ray with the bone break. Once you make a decision and have offered your final opinion regarding how to resolve an issue you have done the first part of your job. Hopefully at some point in time you will know if that decision was the right one. You usually only hear about the wrong ones. By the way those are just other people's opinions anyway.

Rule # 13: Know the Difference between a Battle and the War.

Military logic allows for the loss of many battles while still securing the ultimate victory in war. You have to have the ability to see the big picture. Many times when you are involved with upper management or an account, you have to realize that you can lose one or more battles and that it will be in your best interest. Don't lose sight of your long-term relationships. You have to give a little to get a little.

As a manager, you have to make a conscious decision where to draw the line. You have to read the body language. If you know the person with the trump card is making a stand that you probably cannot win, it might be a sound decision to accept it graciously. As an example, we had a dealer who received the wrong color product for a job that was already delivered. We had no more stock available in the right color. The salesperson located another dealer one hundred miles away who had the correct stock. He drove back and forth to deliver the new inventory to the retailer. We asked the retailer to put the wrong goods on a truck that day, so we could make the proper credit arrangements. He refused to do it, saying he would not take the old stuff out until the end user approved the replacement. The salesperson thought he was unreasonable. The account was our largest in that district.

The dealer called to tell me what morons we were and how this was our problem, not his. Even though we performed miraculously under

24

the circumstances, I recognized that—in no way, shape, or form—we were going to win this argument. The dealer had some valid points. Once I understood the dealer's point of view, I graciously showed him all the empathy that I could muster and did everything in my power to satisfy his needs. I am confident that, in this situation, I had only one correct decision. My evaluation of the problem came about after the initial decision was made. We could have avoided the confrontation if all the players down the line had the chance to recognize the situation for what it was. Yes, the retailer could have agreed to put the mistaken inventory on a truck and return it to our warehouse, but he had his own agenda. Just stay focused on your goals and plans, and put everything together as part of the big picture. Your ultimate goal is to win the war and have a successful year. So here's a tip for you new managers. (By the way, TIPS is an acronym for these words: To Insure Prompt Service.)—"know when to hold 'em and know when to fold 'em."

Rule #14: Don't Be a Yes-Man or Yes-Woman.

Yes-people are individuals who don't like to stir the pot, so to speak. They go along with the company line and are loyal followers. We used to call many of these people "brownnosers." Simply put they had their nose so close to the boss's butt that if the boss stopped short, the tip of their nose would turn brown from coming into contact with that illegal word. By agreeing with everything they were earning their brownie points.

There really is nothing wrong with going along with your supervisor's decisions. You just have to get a feel for when it is the right time to make your stand and fight your battle. I have met many people whose extreme mantra has been "I am not a yes-man" and who take the corresponding action. It seems as though they disagree with everything. You have to decide when to have a dissenting opinion worth exploring. Many times, we make knee-jerk decisions. We don't have enough time to explore all the options. Whenever possible, explore your possibilities. Many times, I have stuck my neck out to champion what I thought was the better way of doing something. I try to temper my feelings, but getting emotional about something is normal.

Be sure you create an environment where people feel free to express their opinions. Open dialogue produces great things. If people trust you, they will feel free to share their ideas. Recognize when the debate has been settled, join hands with the winning side, and be part of the team to push that decision forward.

As an example, a few months ago at our managers' meeting, the regional vice president called me over to the side and said, "I don't want you to argue with me about this, but I have decided not to have your regional dealer convention this year." Now this hit me like a sharp stick in the eye. A wave of information had to be processed in not much more than a few seconds. The regional convention was a casino extravaganza of monumental proportions. The first things that hit me was the impact this would have on the morale of my salespeople, including all the negative repercussions. And how would I break the news to my customer base? How would my competition use this against us? The wheels were spinning furiously in all directions in my mind. After about three seconds, I am sure I had reached my decision as to how to respond. I respect and trust my vice president's ability to make good decisions. He had to have all the facts at his disposal to make this dramatic decision because my regional performance impacts everything he does. He wouldn't have made this decision without consulting me unless he was convinced he had no other choice.

That alone led me to conclude that *the corporation* had some influence here. Why else would he make such a unilateral decision? Now, I could have put on my "I am not a yes-man" persona, but I was experienced enough to recognize the signs. He was crystal clear that it was not up for discussion. My only logical response was to support his position and make the best of a bad situation. Don't be a manager and think for a moment that every decision is based on democratic principles of the majority. Someone has to make the tough decisions. Whatever my opinion might have been, the fact was that the conversation was over. As Alfred Lord Tennyson wrote in "The Charge of the Light Brigade": "Theirs not to reason why, /Theirs but to do or die:/Into the valley of Death/Rode the six hundred." Sometimes, that's all she wrote.

Rule #15: Sales Is Incentive-Driven.

When you decide that sales needs a good shot in the arm, there is nothing like a good old promotion to light some proverbial fires. I believe that this is a good way to pump up business and morale.

Under the right circumstances, promotions can get individuals to respond to the competition. Well-conceived promotions are good managerial tools to spike business for a specific sales period. They should be timely and meaningful. Offering sales performance incentive funds (SPIFs) for performance levels provides great incentives for the success of the promotion.

Be sure you make the incentives realistic and reachable. Measure the results in short increments to ensure everyone is participating. If employees don't seem to want to pursue the incentive, they will lose interest. Your job is to decide what "reasonable" is. We are all reasonable people; that is why we were chosen to be managers.

Do not forget that managers are also incentive-driven. Bonuses and sales rewards are critical in motivating individuals to try to achieve optimal results. There is nothing wrong with being motivated by money. One of your jobs as a manager is to find out what motivates your people. Competition is a great tool for getting results. Don't be afraid to use it. In many ways, you must become an amateur or even professional psychologist. Listen to what these people have to tell you. Learn what makes them tick. The more you understand where they are coming from, the better you will be able to help get them to your destination. Just remember that different strokes for different folks does apply here.

Rule #16: Leave a Paper Trail.

This concept differs considerably from the rule that "if you want a good memory, write it down." I use the term "paper trail" for that old-fashioned tool known as "your file." This term has to do with personnel evaluation for negative and positive reasons. In many cases, sales reviews should be documented quarterly or annually. It is good to put down the many fine things an employee has done in his or her position.

In most cases, however, the real paper trail has to do with people with poor or substandard performance. You are concerned about an individual's performance. You may have addressed it on several occasions in conversation. Now the person has done something, either a singular or cumulative event, which needs to be written up formally. There are different degrees of formal documentation. A short note or just putting something on record can, in many ways, serve the same purpose as a formal letter setting out the chapter and verse of a particular offense. The decision to send out such a note should not be taken lightly. In most cases, it requires a series of events that have led to your conclusion. Decisions of this nature give you the time to discuss the situation with other managers and supervisors to determine what you should do. In very serious situations, you should have someone in management or human resources review the communication before you send it out. This first note is the beginning of a process that may lead you to terminate that employee.

In large corporations like mine, it would be difficult to let a person go without this paper trail. The paper trail is part of the process of identifying a problem and bringing it to the employee's attention. In most cases, your mutual goal will be to correct the problem within a certain time frame. Successfully working this out with the employee is your ultimate goal. You are just going on record that there is a problem. Once an employee receives a letter like this, he or she usually becomes defensive.

There may be times when you initiate this paper trail because you want to start the process of termination. This will be a warning letter for the employee, somewhat in the form of the warning in the punch line "The cat is on the roof."

For those unfamiliar with that story, it is worth telling. A man goes on vacation and while away he gets a call from his best friend, who is watching his house telling him, "Your cat died." "Gee," the man responds, "Couldn't you have broken the news a little more gently? You know how much I loved that cat! Couldn't you have just told me today that my cat is on the roof? "Then you could have called me tomorrow and said my cat fell off the roof and they took her to the animal hospital and she was in pretty bad shape." Then the next day you could have broken the bad news that my dear sweet cat died and I would have been better prepared for it." The friend apologizes for not being thoughtful enough and says he will remember his advice for the future. The next day the friend calls again to say, "Your mother's on the roof." Know how to deliver the message and polish your written communication skills.

Rule #17: Don't Procrastinate.

Today's News Flash—"National Procrastination Week has been postponed until next week."

Once you decide to do something, do it. Strike while the iron is hot. Procrastinating decisions and assignments is dangerous and hazardous to your health. I have been guilty of procrastination. There—I've said it for all the world to hear. I have put it off for too long.

My name is Michael Fishman, and I am a procrastinator. I have been procrastinating writing this book for too long. Once I make a decision, I want to act. I do not want to dwell on putting it off. It is just so easy and comforting to do it tomorrow. Procrastination is an easy way to put off the inevitable.

You might say, "Gee, but I only procrastinate when it comes to the things I don't want to do."

You'll feel better if you do whatever must be done as soon as possible. You are going to have to do it eventually anyway. By doing it in a timely manner, you will clear your mind and do your job better. The old adage "Never put off until tomorrow what you can do today" applies in your work as a manager. Don't underestimate this message. The timeliness of how you do your reports and assignments will reflect on your performance evaluation. It is an integral part of your future success.

Procrastination is a waste of time and time is your most precious commodity. Don't get caught trading your commodities. Serious fines and losses will follow. I don't want to cram anything more into this simple rule.

Rule #18: Try to Make Everyone Part of the Decision.

The title of this chapter has a nice ring to it, but in practice, it is a skill of an accomplished manager. It takes real selling skills to get everyone to be on the same page, especially if they started out in a different chapter. There are times when I failed to get other managers to buy into what I was trying to convey. I listened to what they had to say, but I felt I had the better solution.

Persuading other people to change their minds is often difficult or impossible. If you are the ultimate decision maker, it is your job to have the final word. If, on the other hand, you come up with a solution through persuasion, compromise, and negotiation, you have accomplished your goal. Many people will say, "My mind is made up; don't confuse me with additional information." In many instances, explaining your logic will help people understand and accept your decision even if they are initially lukewarm toward it. Your explanation is a lot better than an attitude that conveys "Hey, it stinks, but that's the way it is."

When new managers call me for advice or my opinion, the first thing I say is, "Do you have a few minutes to discuss this?" They know I am going to give them a long explanation for what might be a simple answer. I want them to understand everything that went into my thinking to reach my conclusion. My second response would be,

"What would you do?" Once I have determined their mind-set, I have a better idea of what they want to do and what I have to do to make them part of the solution.

Get them involved in the whole process. Take them into your confidence. Value their input, and listen to their arguments. Reason with them on every point. Agree to disagree. Do all you can to make them understand your position and why you are taking it. But if they still don't agree with your thinking, they will eventually learn the standard corporate motto that overrides all other logic: "It is what it is."

I recently came up with a new plan to reorganize the sales staff during a down economy. The corporation came up with their own plan that left no room for exceptions. I did my best to show them that, in some areas, my plan had a much better chance of success. We needed some flexibility to adjust to regional differences and needs. Their simple answer was that this is how we have made our decision, and this is how are doing it. It is what it is.

Rule #19: "It ain't over 'til it's over" Applies to Baseball, not Sales.

Let me paint a picture of what this title means.

Yogi Berra was a great Yankee baseball player who had a knack for saying things in a unique, memorable way. I read somewhere that, other than the Bible and Shakespeare, Yogi Berra is the most quoted resource in America.

When Yogi stated, "It ain't over 'til it's over," he was referring to baseball. We have tried to apply that expression to everything else, and it doesn't work. A baseball game is not over until the final out is recorded. You can be losing by ten runs with two out in the ninth inning and still win the game. You basically cannot create the situation where, theoretically, you could not win the game.

I always remember the 1965 New York mayoral election in which William F. Buckley was the Conservative Party candidate. On the eve of the election, he was interviewed on television, where it was pointed out to him that the closing polls had him with only a 20 percent share of the vote. Asked if he could still win the election, he responded, "Theoretically."

The newscaster asked him what he meant by "theoretically," to which Buckley answered, "If I get enough votes."

That was a good enough reply, among others, to get my liberal democrat vote. The best I can recall, he still only received approximately the same 20 percent he was predicted to get the evening before. My point is that for Buckley it wasn't over till the votes were cast.

In all other major sports, there is a time limit that prevents that saying from being a truism. For example, assume in a football game, where the score is 36 to 0, that the team with the lead has the ball with one minute left on the time clock and that the other team has no timeouts. Go home—the outcome of the game is over. You can cite similar situations with basketball and hockey. Baseball is the only American team sport without a time clock. Sales has a time clock. Each week, each month, each quarter—each unit of time is written into the record books. If you have a terrible sales year for the first eleven months—no matter how spectacular the finish—you won't win. You might pull out the month, but you won't pull out the year. You've already lost that.

It's over. As we say, "Stick a fork in it." Recognize it and move on. You have to manage in the present. All your measurements are history lessons. Make your adjustments as they happen. If you are down 50 percent for the month and there is one week left, it is basically over. Don't rely on miracle endings. You can't wait that long to change the outcome."

"What have you done for me lately" is a fact of life in sales. Learn the difference between history and current events. As a manager, you measure your staff's sales performance. After you do that, you'd better have a good plan for what they are going to do tomorrow.

Somebody once asked Yogi what time it was. He responded, "Do you mean right now"?

Rule #20: Know How to Identify Your Priorities.

I will not try to teach you the importance of time management. It is just too self-evident. Take a class. Get a system. Tempus fugit—*time flies*. Time seems to zoom by at rocket speed. One day you wake up, it's Memorial Day—a week later, it's Labor Day.

In our twenty-four-hour day, it is critical that we figure out our priorities and how to maximize the use of our time. It is not a stretch to say that we all feel that with modern technology we are on duty 24/7. You should try to develop a sixth sense and figure out not just what is most important to you but what is most important to the people you work for. LIFO is the acronym in inventory for "Last In First Out." So many times, when I talk to my staff, I say, "The number one priority is blah, blah." A few minutes later, I might say the number one priority is "foo fah." There will be times, as strange as it sounds, when there are multiple number one priorities. You have to figure out in which order you can do them. Train yourself to read the signals. See which items roll downhill the fastest. Write your to-do list. You will not only feel you have accomplished something, but you will actually feel a sense of relief.

Try to avoid multitasking whenever possible. In his book *Crazy Busy*, Dr. Edward Hallowell equates multitasking with trying to play tennis with two balls at the same time. No matter how good a tennis player you are, you will always do better with just one ball in play. I use the acronym OHIO (Only Handle It Once) from that book, which helps me gain about thirty minutes a week. This method is great for reading e-mails, of which I receive an average of at least fifty to sixty each day. Dr. Hallaway recommends three choices for handling e-mail. The basic premise is not to keep it on your screen because you will just be forced to read it over and over again until you decide to do something with it.

Just respond to it, file it, or delete it. The best advice is to delete it. Deleting is such an exhilarating feeling. Don't you feel good every time you do it? It's completion by deletion.

Having nothing remaining on your message screen is divine.

RULE #21: HAVE INTEGRITY.

There is a popular adage that makes a lot of sense to me: "You never get a second chance to make a first impression." That could ring true in many situations; but when it comes to establishing your reputation, you will get multiple chances to prove yourself. As with respect, a good reputation is something we must earn. The way we conduct ourselves when we deal with other members of our business community requires conscientious decisions about social behavior and ethics. It is hard to earn a good reputation, and it is something that depends on others to determine. How they judge you is what counts. Each person can have an opinion that differs from the next person's.

What is even harder to describe is what gives certain people a presence. You might have everyone's respect and a good reputation, but do you have presence? (By the way, just having the title of manager gives you a head start.)

Presence is one of those elusive traits that are difficult to define exactly. It is an aura your entire demeanor generates. Some people say you either have *it*, or you don't have *it*. In my opinion, there are those who can acquire presence with experience. Then again, if you have presence and a good reputation, do you have class? The same can be said for charisma. All of these terms that people apply to other people—a good reputation, respect, presence, class, and charisma—are terms of recognition of, and awe toward, the person. Many people judge you in different ways. Yet there is one constant in all this and one word that will trump all the others. It doesn't require the judgment of others. That word is integrity.

The dictionary defines integrity as a steadfast adherence to a strict, moral ethical code. To me, it is just simply doing the right thing. I was reminded of this word just the other day. One of my managers was telling me about the time his company had been acquired by a larger one, and he was convinced that his job was in danger. All around him members of upper management were getting axed. He was called into the new vice president's office and asked the question, "So what do you bring to the table? What do you offer us?" He thought for a second and then gave a simple two-word answer, "my integrity." He kept his job. This story affected me so much that I added it to the rules to reflect that realization and its importance.

I have also heard a cute story that kind of puts the issue of integrity into perspective. A young boy asks his father if he can tell him the meaning of integrity.

The father says, "Yes, I will be happy to give you an example. You know in our carpet store, Uncle Danny and I are equal partners. That means that everything we make we split fifty-fifty. The other day, an older woman came into our store; and she reminded me so much of my mom, your grandma, that it was scary.

"She explained that she was a widow on Social Security and had saved a hundred dollars to buy a new rug. Her family was coming over for Christmas, and she had the same old rug for thirty years. Because of her fixed income, she couldn't afford a penny more.

"I felt really bad for her, so I took her in the back room and found her a nice remnant in just the exact color and size she wanted. Even though it was marked up for much more, I agreed to let her have it for a hundred bucks, tax included.

"She proceeded to open her bank envelope and hand me a crisp one-hundred dollar bill that I put into my pocket." Since her son was waiting in the car outside, I had one of my guys carry the carpet out the front door and tie it on the roof.

"Just as she was about to exit the store, I put my hand in my pocket and realized that she had mistakenly given me two one-hundred dollar bills instead of one. The crisp new bills had evidently stuck together.

"Now I had to make a quick decision that will answer your question about integrity. My choices were to keep the second one-hundred dollar bill for myself or split it with my fifty-fifty partner, Uncle Danny."

Now I hope you realize that I intentionally gave you a humorous example of someone who has absolutely no integrity. Remember that the one thing—you can never compromise is your integrity.

All good managers must always show the leadership to do the right thing no matter how hard it may seem. Don't be left out.

Rule #22: Don't Be Afraid to Show Your Emotions.

Some people know that I have a tendency to use off-color words in the course of some of my ramblings. I use them for effect and to add color and emotion to what I am trying to convey. Using such words makes the message so much juicier. I consciously choose to do it.

Emotions, however, are a bit different. Sometimes, they just spew out as a natural reaction. The same situation can generate emotions that range between great laughter in one context and considerable indignation or anger in another context. I am not talking about condoning someone's actions if that person belongs in an anger management course. I am not talking about accepting abusive behavior. I am not talking about exhibiting road rage or going postal. I am talking about reasonable reactions to a set of circumstances, in which you need to demonstrate your happiness, displeasure, or another emotion that aligns with your thoughts and feelings about a matter. Let people know how you feel. You can be cool, calm, and collected; but you have to be able to communicate your feelings so people know where you stand.

Being cool is still cool after all these years. But you must be confrontational. Whether this comes naturally to you or you cringe at the thought of it, it doesn't make a difference. You must confront issues at times.

We are dealing with people and events that no matter what the business might be, to those involved, emotions can run high. Confrontations and emotions seem to go hand in hand.

One method of confrontation may include a simple request to discuss something with someone. "Do you mind if I tell you something you may not be aware of?" might be the question you need to start that conversation. As managers, we have to confront or discuss unpleasant or negative things with our staff and create a scenario that demands an answer. You must decide how diplomatically or bluntly you choose to initiate the confrontation. Confrontations put people on the spot and often involve emotions. Try to predict all the possibilities your confrontation can elicit. More often than not, laying all your cards out on the table is a good thing. You've got the deck in your hands, so deal the cards. Sometimes you have to act like the boss. One day it will come naturally, and you won't have to act anymore. But I am officially giving you permission and making it legal to get pissed off.

Rule #23: The Customer Is Always Right (Unless They Are Proven Wrong).

I actually was going to end the page right here. I wouldn't have been too far off course. If you start out with this basic rule, you will always be a better decision maker. The unwritten rule in business—the way I was taught—is that we give our customers the benefit of the doubt. Unless there is a *smoking gun* to indicate the customer is wrong, go with the premise that the customer is always right until proven otherwise. And even then, in many cases, you would be wise to go with the *always* part. My first confrontation with a customer provides some perspective on that maxim and demonstrates the proof one needs to prove the customer wrong.

I was a relatively new salesperson when I had my first real confrontation. I had gotten a message to call one of my customers, and—in line with my training—I returned that call as soon as I got to a pay phone. It was a small store, but I still politely announced who I was and asked what was up.

"Do you know who the freak you are talking to?" the customer roared. (I apologize for using the language that follows, but I am just repeating exactly what the customer said. (If I didn't give you an accurate description of his language you could miss the value of this story and the colorful character involved. (I will substitute the word freak for the English Law acronym of the street slang f-word that is the definition of rape, For Unlawful Carnal Knowledge). This customer was a tough-looking guy, and his store was well connected.

"I had to find," the customer continued, "about your freaking product Tripoli from another dealer because you didn't give me that sample binder. Do you think I am some shit little store? If you want to do business with me, you better make sure I get every freakin' sample that your company carries." This customer had previously given me no business during my first six months with this company.

It is important to note that, in that time and place, we gave out free sample binders to any dealer we deemed viable to sell that product. I personally probably had enough books for half the customers in my territory. I could realistically service about one hundred stores with any regularity out of my two hundred.

It is also important to note that I did visit this account regularly even though for my first six months on the job he had given me zero business.

To make matters even worse, the last time I was there I got a parking ticket. Being a street-smart young lad, I recognized that he was pissed off; and he was venting it at me. As I listened to his screaming, I was looking at my sample inventory cards that clearly indicated I had, in fact, placed that sample binder in his store. (I was extremely methodical in my record keeping and ultra-organized.) But the customer is always right, so I was very apologetic and made arrangements to drop off the sample binder he wanted on the following day.

When I arrived at the store, the owner saw me coming in. Just as I started to walk toward him, I noticed a pile of welcome mat-size rugs were offered for sale at a dollar each. In that pile of doormats, I saw an orange doormat that was the same distinctive bright orange top swatch and style as the Tripoli sample book I was carrying into the store.

While he was still watching me, I reached down and pulled out the small orange rug. There next to my company logo was the name *Tripoli* clearly printed on the back. This meant that he had taken apart my free sample binder and was selling the large top swatch as a doormat for a dollar—something dealers would do only after a product was discontinued.

I walked up to his desk and dropped the sample on top of some papers he was working on. As cool as a cucumber, I said, "Here's the freakin' Tripoli sample you said you never got. If all you want my sample books for is to sell off the top swatches, you can just shove them up your ass instead." With that, I turned around and headed for the door.

Now I don't know where I got the guts to be that confrontational, but I certainly had the smoking gun to bolster my courage.

The dealer followed me into the street and started muttering all kinds of excuses and apologies. We went back into his store; and after much conversation, he gave me a nice order for inventory. From that day forward, we got along fine because we spoke the same language.

With that said, can we really say the customer is always right? It might be interesting to note that this dealer was involved in one of the largest money heists in U.S. history. The movie *Goodfellas* dealt with some of that subject matter. He was the only person, to my knowledge, convicted of that crime, and he served nine years in prison for taking the hit.

Of course every situation depends on every new set of circumstances. It is rare when the real facts make the answers come out and bite you.

At one point in my career, I moved away from the New York City area into the farmlands of northern Connecticut. It was kind of like going from mobsters to lobsters. My biggest account in Brooklyn was owned by Sammy "The Bull" Gravano and Paul Castellano. These were two of the most famous mobsters of our generation. Throw in the Bonano family store and a host of other lesser known names and you can get an idea of how street-smart I really had to be. Hell, I should probably write a book.

Rule #24: When You Come to a Fork in the Road, Take It.

The title to this rule comes from another phrase attributed to Yogi Berra. This rule is meaningful to me as it applies to the decision-making process. I mean, sometimes you are just going to have to make a decision. It's kind of like "Shit or get off the pot." You can go left, or you can go right. You might have examined everything you can possibly examine. You might have sought out the opinions of others. But you are at the crossroads, and the traffic is backing up behind you.

Try to listen to everyone honking behind you. You have one foot in and one foot out the door. Make a decision. Go with your best instincts. With the law of averages, you should be half right.

Sometimes, people will advise you that the worst decision is not to make a decision. But if you make a decision not to do something, then your choice of inaction should be because that is your decision. In sports, we often hear the best trade was the one they didn't make. That's okay. But make a conscious decision to make the decision and move on. Don't be afraid to make unpopular decisions when you think you are right. Don't be afraid to make a decision because people will second-guess you. Just don't be afraid of doing your job.

If you have the ability at some point in time to examine your decisions, it would serve you well to assess how you did. Was a decision right or wrong? What could you have done differently? Remember that hindsight is twenty-twenty. Simple forks in the road are a little better. They are fifty-fifty.

Rule #25: Try to Never Make a Decision That Can Be Overturned.

I saved this rule for last on purpose.

What can be worse than when you finally make a difficult decision you think you have the authority to make and you have to renege on it? It is a blow to your credibility. Not only is it embarrassing, but it can result in a domino effect of bad side effects if other people depended on the finality of your decision.

Not all decisions will be low risk and hard to overturn. Your organizational structure will not always be what you thought it was. Be prepared for surprises.

I was once involved in a salary negotiation and had made a deal with a candidate for a job based on my understanding of what I could offer in my package. When my supervisor advised me that he wanted to reduce the offer, I vehemently tried to explain what led me to my decision. It was a very small difference, but it was a difference that put me in an awkward position. I wasn't getting the support I had hoped for.

The new hire still accepted my revised deal even though it left me feeling powerless, embarrassed, and defeated. I made the decision that I would never knowingly put myself in that position again. I would always check and recheck my boundaries whenever I thought I was on the boundaries of my authority. Now I often use phrases such as "subject to corporate approval," "subject to credit approval," and subject to anything else that may pose a threat to my decision.

In the last weeks of writing these twenty-five rules, something happened that made me reflect on the adage "Never say never." My company had just developed a new organizational game plan, and we had carefully done our due diligence and received our go-ahead. Everyone was in perfect agreement that we had developed a good plan with considerable potential. Two months later, the corporate office decided on a different game plan that made our directives null and void. I now had to start notifying the people involved and, in many cases, pull back their new positions.

The realities of business and profit are paramount in any for-profit organization. It was a very difficult time for me. I am close to my people, and they trust my leadership. Sometimes, I liken our sales teams on the streets to platoons in foxholes. We are involved in our own form of hand-to-hand combat with our competition. There are times it seems as if we are fighting by the Marquis of Queensbury rules with sixteen-ounce gloves where the competitors somehow get to use brass knuckles. It is important for our team members to watch each other's back and stand behind our team's decisions, whether we agree or disagree. Once a decision is made, we have to go out together and make it work. These are situations that will weigh heavily upon you. As a manager you will have to work through these emotions and focus on your integrity. Hopefully those that you work with have the same standards.

If you are empowered to make the decision and you make it, I will back you. As an example, some mangers made some decisions on two separate occasions that made me cringe a little. Each decision had to do with opening new accounts in areas where there were existing dominant accounts. These decisions involved complicated marketing strategies that would definitely ruffle some feathers and possibly lead to serious repercussions from our dealer base. The managers discussed the circumstances with everyone involved and, after gathering the facts as they knew them, were empowered to make the final decision because they were in charge of those districts.

Once they started to put these plans in play and open these new accounts, the shit hit the fan. (There is really no better way to say it.)

As I had predicted, the dealers involved were outraged far worse than I could have ever imagined. Our damage control management teams on every level were called into play to put out or mitigate the raging fires. They were painful confrontations, but we all survived but still have some scars to show for it.

Even though I was not strongly in favor of the decisions my managers made to put us in this situation, I did everything in my power to convey a unified front and justify our position. I gave them my full support. I watched their backs.

Learning to become a Street-Smart manager is not an easy job.

When you ruffle some feathers just remember, "Birds of a feather flock together."

Tie it All Together.

This is just some advice I would like to add to my twenty-five rules. They are simple ways I try to conduct my business life. You may have a different management job, and you might come from a different culture or lifestyle. If that is the case, you can choose to do whatever works best for you; and this advice may not apply.

In my world of business, dressing professionally is a very important aspect of how your clients perceive you. I will give an interesting story that stands out in my memory, which might make this more crystal clear.

In 1985, I was highly recruited and headhunted by a major corporation within my industry to manage one of their regions. The corporation gave me a powerful offer, and I accepted the position. About three weeks into my new job, we participated at an industry expo in Atlanta. I had made plans and was looking forward to hooking up with some of my old cronies to celebrate my promotion. Unfortunately, my new employers told me that my attendance was requested at a testimonial dinner that evening because they needed one more body to fill their table.

I was not thrilled by this turn of events. I contacted my friends and postponed our meeting until later that night. After working our showroom floor from 8:00 AM until 6:00 PM, I went back to my hotel room to shower and change out of my sweaty suit and tie and put on a fresh, brand-new outfit, including a black silk shirt and hankie. I went to the dinner and wound up sitting between the chairman of the board of directors and the president of the corporation. These were not the chattiest, small-talk guys I had ever met.

The testimonial dinner was starting to become a very long, boring evening. The strange thing was that it also became a testimonial dinner for me more than the guy on the stage. All evening long, prestigious members of our industry kept coming to our table to congratulate me on my new position and to tell anyone within earshot about how lucky the company was to get a person of my talent and reputation. I could not have planned it better even if I had tried.

The next morning I met for breakfast with the same vice presidents, who had hired me, and said that the chairman of the board had asked them who "this guy Mike Fishman" was. The vice presidents explained to him again about my new position—something he was already well aware of.

"Well he wasn't wearing a tie," the chairman responded.

Now I was kind of caught off guard because I had been thinking that, after fifteen or twenty people had come by our table to sing my praises, all he could comment on was that I wasn't wearing a tie.

All I said was, "Hey, I am only here three weeks and the chairman of the board already knows my name."

This will seem even more of an enigma to anyone who knows me. At a minimum standard of dress, a shirt and a tie are definite requirements for me. Most people think I go to sleep wearing a tie. Wearing colorful, bold ties has always been one of my trademarks. You can wear the same old blue blazer or tired gray suit a hundred times, but add a bright new tie, and you will still get a compliment.

Wearing a tie at business meetings was such an important way of life back then that one major company threatened one of their superstar salesmen that, if he didn't wear a tie to their meeting, he would be fired. So he wore a tie. Unfortunately, he wore only his underwear instead of his suit. His employer had no sense of humor, and he was fired. My rule of thumb is that, if you are going to be with customers, men have to wear, at least, a dress shirt and tie. Women managers have to wear an appropriate professional outfit.

In the workplace, managers should look the part and set the tone. It is far better to be a little overdressed than underdressed. Today when we plan to have meetings, the announcement often comes with a dress code that sets the minimum guidelines. The new buzzwords are "business casual," which is usually defined even further in the memo so that men and women attendees know what is deemed appropriate. It is usually a dress-down standard.

Unfortunately, some people don't have a clue with respect to looking your best. I had a meeting of territory managers at a hotel a few years ago with the standard "business casual" attached to the e-mail notice. Two salespeople actually arrived in Bermuda shorts and beach-style flip-flops. I let them know that this was inappropriate, and I now have to spell out in explicit detail what my definition of business casual is. It seems bizarre to me that people actually think this would have been acceptable. I personally always want to look professional and successful.

On another front, I also think it is imperative to mind your p's and q's. This refers back to Colonial times when tavern bartenders kept a tabulated record on a chalkboard, of how many pints and quarts of rum and ale you drank so that you could settle the tab at the end of the night. Too often, I have seen important people embarrass themselves by getting "shit-faced" at some public business social gathering. If you think this has in any way had a positive influence on your reputation, you are sadly mistaken. Watch what you do out there. I'll drink to that.

Conclusion

So you wanted to be the manager? It may not be as easy as you think. In my career as a sales manager and general sales manager, I know I have interviewed more than five hundred candidates for sales and management positions. I am sure I have hired or promoted over one hundred people from that group. My first conclusion is that I am a far better interviewer now than I was at first. This experience is something that is hard to pass along. I know I have a much higher rate of success in my selections now than in the past. I still make mistakes. Like any good doctor, I am still practicing my trade. Maybe if I had concentrated more on training these people, as I do now, my success rate would have been much higher than in the earlier days. But I wasn't as wise as I am today.

When it comes to people seeking to become sales managers, very few are even prepared for the interview process. Some are clueless about how to answer the simplest questions. Some still will probably get the job. One of my strongest beliefs is that hiring and training the right people are the most important jobs a manager has. It is easy for someone to make that statement, but do you have that ability? What makes you think you have that type of talent to find and develop talent? It is a skill you must work on and can only develop over time. Many new managers learn the hard way, and so will those they manage. It seems that everyone thinks that anyone can be the manager. In reality, almost anyone can become a manager, but not everyone will be a good one.

I have found it very difficult to limit myself to only twenty-five things that I have learned over all these years. How did I figure out what to eliminate? As with everything else we do as managers, I had to decide which ones were the most important to me. I tried to limit this message so that it would be easy to read and even easier to remember. Eventually, you will develop your own bag of tricks. Maybe some wisdom from this book will make it possible for you not to have to start from scratch. That expression, by the way, comes from horse racing when in the old days they would scratch a line in the dirt to mark where the race would start. If you can get out of the gate with a head start, your odds of success will be greatly enhanced. You might even become the favorite to succeed.

The new world of business is in the fast lane. I like to refer to this new world by that simple oxymoron *organized chaos*, where it's just a wide-open race and anything goes. Everything is changing at such a rapid rate of speed that, in so many ways, long-term planning has been substituted with day trading. Technology has brought micromanagement to a new level of detail that borders on the forensic in its magnification. Managers have to stay ahead of the curve.

You must learn as soon as possible that there is no place to hide. Crap will roll down that hill faster than you can imagine. Through all these changes and challenges, the opportunity to succeed is still as great as ever before. I believe that to be happy in your career, you must figure out what you like to do and find someone willing to pay you to do it. There will never be a substitute for being in the right place at the right time. Once you recognize when the opportunity presents itself, you don't want to blow it. Maybe the key to your kingdom is right in front of your eyes. Just be sure you play by the rules.

Thanks for reading my book.